HOMAGE TO JOHN CLARE

HOMAGE TO JOHN CLARE:

A Poetical and Critical Correspondence

Peter Neumeyer

Foreword by William Meredith

Peregrine Smith, Inc.
SALT LAKE CITY
1980

To Helen

Copyright © 1979 by Peregrine Smith, Inc.

All rights reserved. No part of this book may be used or reproduced by any means without written permission from the publisher.

Library of Congress Cataloging in Publication Data

Neumeyer, Peter, 1929–
    Homage to John Clare.
        1. Clare, John, 1793–1864, in fiction, drama, poetry, etc. I. Title.
PS3564.E8465H6   811'.5'4   79-20609
ISBN 0-87905-056-X

Manufactured in the United States of America

FOREWORD

Opposite a letter to Eliza Phillips, written by John Clare some four years after he had committed himself to an insane asylum, Eliza Phillips being either an imaginary woman or one existing in a relationship wholly fantasized by Clare, and a letter in which Clare believes himself to be the prize-fighter Ben Caunt, and says he is writing new cantos of *Don Juan* and *Child Harold*—opposite this letter, Peter Neumeyer has placed a poem containing these lines:

Three things I say:
I am a fighter who has never known defeat;
I write not often words like this, but you I love;
I, beside myself, guiding my hand, write Byron's poem.

Three things I say, in all, are one:
I fight all fighters, yet none comes.
I love a figment I know well, who never was.
My heart's own poem is not my own.

You think I do not know these things
You think poor Clare is mad,
    thinks he is Caunt, he loves a shadow, writes another's poems,
    and knows not he is small, is modest married, versifies with limp.

And I reply
I tell you I
AM FEARLESS
PASS AMONG MY FOES

It is the kind of commentary that imaginative writing can make and criticism cannot.

Homage to John Clare is not criticism, except, as the author says, in its intention to shed light on its subject. But neither is it one of those works of the creative imagination, springing from a major text, which *confront* their models, a genre we see a good deal of as our culture trails self-consciously off: Anouilh's *Antigone*, Stoppard's *Rosencrantz and Guildenstern are Dead*, Auden's *The Sea and the Mirror*, Gardner's *Grendel* suggest the range of this genre.

Neumeyer's *Homage* is a more self-effacing, apparently more passive response than the works just mentioned. Here the modest spirit of John Clare is invoked in a sequence of "flyeing mirrors," poems which respond in dialogue to Clare's poems and prose. The frame of these bright pairings is the almost-effaced character of Peter Neumeyer, who disclaims the contemporary voice which would assert (as all the authors above assert) counter-originality. No modern poet I can think of, producing a work of his own in his role of poet, would resist some projection of his own life and ego. Even in the last poem, Neumeyer simply subsumes again the autobiographical character of John Clare in the pronoun *I*. It is one of the many indications we have that the author's love for Clare is so attentive as to be quite trustworthy. An enthusiast who has understood Clare, Neumeyer reveals that understanding by emulating the humility of his model. Homage may involve self-discovery, but by definition it is not an act of self-aggrandizement.

An immediate advantage of Neumeyer's deference is to be seen in the diction he has chosen. He seems to confine himself chiefly to the language and poetic effects of Clare, as Clare had confined himself to a language which originated in the world of his poems.

For a long time, Clare was thought to have used a naively archaic language out of ignorance, as Emily Dickinson was thought to have used dissonant rhymes out of clumsiness. But at least since Arthur Symons' edition of Clare in 1908, Geoffrey Grigson writes, "Clare has been transformed from 'peasant-poet' into poet."

It is no longer possible to ascribe Clare's special language to limited reading or to rural poverty. He said acute things about Keats, he parodied Wordsworth, he imitated Byron. It seems to me likely that he wrote quite deliberately in a language still to be heard in the rural culture he loved and lamented. He wrote in a language that had stayed with its objects, as Enclosure and Commerce and The City imperiled those objects and created an artificial tongue. If there is archaism here, it is more social than linguistic. Clare heard how the language of country people conserved things as they were, conserved the values he found congenial. The language of badgers and wrens, snails, and hedgehogs, was to him what Marianne Moore claimed for honest cats and dogs. Clare must have heard this and instinctively stood up for rural language against a language of urban abstractions. (His eccentricity is another matter: he did not receive much useful criticism or any sense of cultural resonance for his poetry, and he was mad when he wrote much of it. The wonder should be, how little it is marred by its eccentricity.)

What he once wrote to his publisher—Keats' publisher too—about Keats is instructive. He faults Keats for letting his eye be drawn away from a natural scene to "a constant allusion or illusion to Grecian mythology.... When he speaks of woods, Dryads & Fawns are sure to follow...His descriptions of scenery are often very fine, but as it is the case with other inhabitants of great cities, he often described nature as she appeared to his fancies & not as he would have described her had he witnessed the things he describes...." These seem to be the observations of a careful reader who has his own misgivings about the style of a contemporary master. Readers of Clare and of this book will see how closely his language has "witnessed the things he describes."

So it was natural that Peter Neumeyer would foreswear overtly modern practices and with them, probably, the claim that these are important modern poems. They are an important modern commentary, free of a particular kind of provincialism. His language refers itself to John Clare as nicely as Clare's language refers itself to its objects. If an artist is good enough—and in a world of well-developed egoism in the arts, this is rare—if an artist is good enough, the poem so conceived will be true to the character of its object. The poem will get out of the way of its subject with the same grace that a fine string quartet gets out of Beethoven's way.

Peter Neumeyer seems to me to have gotten out of the way of this extraordinary poet, allowing us to converse with John Clare because we have heard one of our own contemporaries speak with him accurately and familiarly.

William Meredith

ACKNOWLEDGEMENTS

The author and publisher wish to thank the copyright holders who have kindly given permission for the use of extracts from copyrighted material. The publishers have endeavored to trace all copyright holders, but if any have been overlooked, they will be pleased to make the necessary arrangements.

A number of these poems appeared originally in *Quarry West*, number six (Santa Cruz), and are reprinted by permission.

Sources and Abbreviations

J. C., *Des.*	John Clare, *Poems Descriptive of Rural Life & Scenery*. London: Taylor & Hessey, 1820.
J. C., *Later Poems*	*The Later Poems of John Clare*, ed. Eric Robinson and Geoffrey Summerfield. Manchester University Press, 1964.
J. C., *Letters*	*The Letters of John Clare*, ed. J. W. and Anne Tibble. New York: Barnes and Noble, 1970.
J. C., *Mad.*	*Poems of John Clare's Madness*, ed. G. Grigson. London: Routledge and Kegan Paul, 1949.
J. C., *Prose*	*The Prose of John Clare*, ed. J. W. and Anne Tibble. London: Routledge and Kegan Paul, 1951.
J. C., *Selections*	*Clare: Selected Poems and Prose*, ed. Eric Robinson and Geoffrey Summerfield. Oxford University Press, 1966.
J. C., *Sel. Poems*, G.	*Selected Poems of John Clare*, ed. G. Grigson. Cambridge: Harvard University Press, 1950; also, London: Routledge and Kegan Paul.
J. C., *Shepherd's Cal.*	John Clare, *The Shepherd's Calendar*, ed. Eric Robinson and Geoffrey Summerfield. Oxford University Press, 1973.
T., *Life*	J. W. and Anne Tibble, *John Clare: A Life*. Totowa, N.J.: Rowman and Littlefield, 1972.
	Mark Storey. *The Poetry of John Clare: a critical introduction*. New York: St. Martin's Press, 1974.
	Janet M. Todd. *In Adam's Garden: A Study of John Clare*. Gainesville: University of Florida Press, 1973.

INTRODUCTION

I have heard John Clare's voice, and I have grown fond of him. And so I have wanted to answer him, to express my affection in a poetical Homage, and to carry on a correspondence with John Clare, wherever he may be.

John Clare was a poor, rural poet of nineteenth century England who, undoubtedly influenced by his isolation and what he read, wrote frequently as though he were living in the eighteenth century. He lived long, loved frequently, sometimes surely well. He showed early signs of madness in the 1820s, and was institutionalized from 1837 until his death in 1864. Many of his manuscripts remain to this day scrambled, not all deciphered, and by no means all published.[1] In his periods of delusion, he wrote long poems thinking he was Byron, many poems that are a muddle, and many, many which see God's world clearly, keenly, with compassion, but without false sentiment. Clare's best poems, like "The Badger," and "I am," are, in fact, recognized and frequently anthologized. And, notwithstanding the criticism that Clare "has of late been over-praised,"[2] we cannot dismiss lightly the fact that Clare attracted the attention of John Middleton Murry, Edmund Blunden, C. Day Lewis, and Robert Graves. Scholarship, too, proceeds on Clare at a deliberate pace.[3] And even a modest measure of popular success has come his way in the recent production by the Folger Theatre Group, Washington, D.C., of Edward Bond's play, *The Fool*.[4]

But the real clue that Clare is not a man to be dismissed lies in the fact that he has remained to several of our own more thoughtful poets a haunting, if somewhat secret, touchstone. Sandra McPherson, Jon Anderson, and Mark Halperin have written to John Clare.[5] But better known, perhaps, is Theodore Roethke's evocation of Clare. Roethke puts him in good—and proper—company:

Heard in a Violent Ward

In Heaven, too
You'd be institutionalized.
But that's all right,—
If they let you eat and swear
With the likes of Blake,
And Christopher Smart,
And that sweet man, John Clare.[6]

John Clare lived later than one would guess from reading his poetry. He was born in 1793, in the Midlands, in the small village of Helpstone, Northants, west of Peterborough. Clare himself has given testimony of the almost Edenic joy of his childhood years, suggesting also that even in those earliest days he had been on a private and an individual quest:

> I had plenty of leisure but it was the leisure of solitude for my sundays were demanded to be spent in the fields at horse or cow tending my whole summer was one days employment as it were in the fields I grew so much into the quiet love of nature's preserves that I was never easy but when I was in the fields passing my sabbaths and leisure with the shepherds & herdboys as fancy's prompted sometimes playing at marbles on the smooth-beaten sheeptracks or leapfrog among the thymy molehills sometimes running among the corn to get the red & blue flowers for cockades to play at soldiers or running into the woods to hunt strawberries or stealing peas in churchtime when the owners were safe to boil at the gypseys fire who went half-shares at our stolen luxury we heard the bells chime but the fields was our church & we seemd to feel a religious poetry in our haunts . . . .
> I lovd this solitary disposition from a boy...& my curiosity urgd me to steal an opportunity to explore it that morning I had imagind that the world's end was at the orizon & that a days journey was able to find it so I went on with my heart full of hope's pleasures & discoverys expecting when I got to the brink of the world that I coud look down like looking into a large pit & see into its secrets the same as I believd I coud see heaven by looking into the water....
>
> (J. C., *Prose*, pp. 11–13.)[7]

But during Clare's life, the idyll came to an end. The eighteenth and early part of the nineteenth century saw the enclosure, the parcelling out and the fencing in of what had for centuries been the common lands. The use of these open lands had accounted considerably for the independence and self-sufficiency of English yeomanry. As the land became pieced and enclosed, removed from the common weal, the sense of independence and self-worth of hitherto self-sufficient English small farmers was undermined, and patterns of work, patterns of leisure, and age-old relationships among families toward each other and toward the land were disrupted. And, it certainly seemed to Clare as though old customs, old lore, were brutally extirpated. One may contemplate the dislocation that must have been wrought in Clare's life by such major economic shifts, when even a very slight uprooting, in this instance a four mile move, in 1832, from Helpstone to Northborough, was a traumatic upheaval:

from The Flitting

Ive left my own old home of homes
Green fields and every pleasant place
The summer like a stranger comes
I pause and hardly know her face
I miss the hazels happy green
The blue bells quiet hanging blooms
Where envy's sneer was never seen
Where staring malice never comes

I miss the heath its yellow furze
Molehills and rabbit tracks that lead
Through beesom ling and teazel burrs
That spread a wilderness indeed
The woodland oaks and all below
That their white powdered branches shield
The mossy pads—the very crow
Croaked music in my native fields

I sit me in my corner chair
That seems to feel itself from home
I hear bird music here and there
From awthorn hedge and orchard come
I hear but all is strange and new
—I sat on my old bench in June
The sailing puddocks shrill 'peelew'
Oer royce wood seemed a sweeter tune
(J. C., *Selections*, pp. 196-197.)

Clare himself had always lived in rural poverty—a poverty deepening as his family grew, his wits blurred, and time progressed. There was a brief flurry of what promised to be fame, and he did go to London for several visits, albeit with trepidation:

...I had learned some fearful disclosures of the place [London] he [Burkhardt, a London jeweller] used to caution me if ever I happend to go to be on my guard as if I once lost my way I shoud sure lose my life as the street Ladys would inveigle me into a fine house where I shoud never be seen agen & he describd the pathways on the street as full of trapdoors which dropd down as soon as

pressd on with the feet & spring in their places after the unfortunate countryman had fallen into the deep hole... were he woud be robd & murderd & thrown into boiling cauldrons kept continually boiling for that purpose & his bones sold to the doctors...I kept a continual lookout & fancied every lady I met a decoyer....
(J. C., *Prose*, p. 81.)

Though for a short time Clare was lionized in London, his aspirations for literary recognition were soon disappointed. It was not long before he returned to dire rural poverty and to demanding physical labor. He did marry, one Martha Turner (referred to often as Patty) by whom he had nine children. As early as 1831 Clare noted the insanity inexorably overtaking him. In 1835 he wrote Dr. Darling (the same doctor who bled John Keats, and who, as a friend of Keat's and Clare's publisher, Taylor, ministered without charge to John Clare):

MY DEAR DR DARLING   [Autumn 1835]

I write to tell you I am very unwell & though I cannot describe my feelings well I will tell you as well as I can—sounds affect me very much & things evil as well [as] good thoughts are continually rising in my mind I cannot sleep for I am asleep as it were with my eyes open & I feel chills come over me & a sort of nightmare awake ...I do assure you I am very unwell & cannot keep my mind as it were for I wish to read & cannot...

Yours sincerely
JOHN CLARE

I fear I shall be worse & worse ere you write to me for I have been out for a walk & can scarcely bear up against my fancys or feelings
(J. C., *Letters*, pp. 283-284.)

Two years later, in 1837, John Clare voluntarily entered Matthew Allen's private asylum in Epping Forest. And here, from the asylum, Clare wrote letters to his wife, Patty, as well as to Mary Joyce—or to the memory of Mary Joyce—his childhood sweetheart, whom he could not marry, probably because of her father's objections. Much later, long after Mary Joyce's death, when Clare was far gone in his madness, the name of Mary Joyce sparkles in Clare's confused mind and in his verses. At times he imagined that he was married both to Mary Joyce and to his actual wife, and that he had been incarcerated for bigamy. Here is a letter written, probably in 1841, addressed to Mary Joyce, who had died in 1838, in which Clare makes reference to Martha Turner—"Patty"—his legal wife:

> MY DEAREST MARY
>
> As This Will Be My Last Letter To You Or Any One Else—Let My Stay In Prison Be As Long Or As Short As It May—I Will Write To You & My Dear Patty In The Same Letter[8]

Another, to his wife:

> MY DEAR WIFE
>
> I have not written to you a long while but here I am in the land of Sodom where all the peoples brains are turned the wrong way... You might come & fetch me away for I think I have been here long enough I write this in a green meadow... The confusion & roar of Mill-dams & locks is sounding very pleasant while I write it & its a very beautiful evening—the meadows are greener that [sic] usual after the shower & the meadows are brimful I think it is about two years since I was first sent up to this Hell & not allowed to go out of the gates—There never was a more disgraceful deception than this place.
>
> Keep yourselves happy & comfortable & love one another...
>
> (J. C., *Letters*, pp. 293, 299.)

Although Dr. Allen's asylum was a pleasant and an agreeable refuge, Clare escaped from it in 1841, walking the eighty miles home in four days. Of this walk, he has left a vivid and a moving account. The first night on the road he slept soundly, but the night was troubled:

> ...had a very uneasy dream I thought my first wife lay on my left arm & somebody took her away from my side which made me wake up rather unhappy I thought as I woke somebody said "Mary" but nobody was near.... I was compleatly foot-foundered & broken down when I had got about half way through the town a gravel causeway invited me to rest myself so I lay down & nearly went to sleep & a young woman... came out of a house & said "poor creature" & another more elderly said "O he shams" But when I got up the latter said "O no he don't" as I hobbled along very lame....
>
> (J. C., *Prose*, pp. 245, 249.)

And the arrival at his old home was, of course, a bitter disappointment too. Clare's dream had been correct:

> July 24, 1841. Returned home out of Essex & found no Mary her & her family are nothing to me now—though she herself was once the dearest of all—& how can I forget (J. C., *Prose*, p. 244.)

Later in that same year, 1841, Clare was certified insane, and from 1841 to 1864 (the year before the birth of Yeats) he lived out his long life in the Northampton General Lunatic Asylum, where he was gently cared for and where he wrote voluminously, constantly.

To the more than two decades Clare spent in the asylum, we may trace an extraordinary poetical outpouring—a vast amount of truly terrible writing, but also enchanting lyrics in which, finally, Clare's thorough familiarity with folk lyrics and with Elizabethan song was put to good effect. To these same years we owe some of Clare's most transcendent writings, as well as the strange poems, "Child Harold," and "Don Juan." Periodically, Clare was under the illusion that he was the poet, Byron—or Lord Nelson, or the Duke of Wellington, or the prize-fighter, Ben Caunt.[9]

Clare's asylum writings are the copious products of a fertile and, in a sense, a *tempered*, mind, confused increasingly as time progressed, but lucid on occasion, especially in the earlier years. The poems vary enormously, Clare writing in every humor, with longing, with lyricism, with regret, at times scurrilously—in the manner of Burns's *Merry Muses*—and, on occasion, with heart-breaking despair.

from "Child Harold"

My life hath been one love—no blot it out
My life hath been one chain of contradictions
Madhouses Prisons wh-re shops—never doubt
But that my life hath had some strong convictions
That such was wrong—religion makes restrictions
I would have followed—but life turned a bubble
And clumb the giant stile of maledictions
They took me from my wife and to save trouble
I wed again and made the error double

Yet abscence claims them both and keeps them too
And locks me in a shop in spite of law
Among a low lived set and dirty crew
Here let the Muse oblivions curtain draw
And let man think—for God hath often saw
things here too dirty for the light of day
For in a madhouse there exists no law—

Now stagnant grows my too refined clay
I envy birds their wings to flye away

. . . .

How beautifull this hill of fern swells on
So beautifull the chappel peeps between
The hornbeams—with its simple bell—alone
I wander here hid in a palace green
Mary is abscent—but the forest queen
Nature is with me—morning noon and gloaming
I write my poems in these paths unseen
And when among these brakes and beeches roaming
I sigh for truth and home and love and woman
(J. C., *Later Poems*, pp. 40-41.)

from "Don Juan"

Childern are fond of sucking sugar candy
And maids of sausages—the larger the better
Shopmen are fond of good sigars and brandy
And I of blunt—and if you change the letter
To C or K it would be quite as handy
And throw the next away—but I'm your debtor
For modesty—yet wishing nought between us
I'd hawl close to a she as vulcan did to venus

. . . .

I wish prince Albert on his german journey
I wish the Whigs were out of office and
Pickled in law books of some good attorney
For ways and speeches few can understand
They'll bless ye when in power—in prison scorn ye
And make a man rent his own house and land—
I wish prince Alberts queen was undefiled
—and every man could get his *wife* with child

I wish the devil luck with all my heart
As I would any other honest body
His bad name passes bye me like a f--t
Stinking of brimstone—then like a whisky toddy
We swallow sin which seems to warm the heart
—There's no imputing any sin to God—he
Fills hell with work—and is'n't it a hard case
To leave old whigs and give to hell the carcass
(J. C., *Later Poems*, pp. 85-87.)

For somewhat improved quality, consider another poem from the asylum years:

Winter

How blasted nature is, the scene is winter
The Autumn withered every branch
Leaves drop, and turn to colourless soil
Ice shoots i' splinters at the river Bridge
And by and bye all stop—
White shines the snow upon the far hill top
Nature's all withered to the root, her printer
To decay that neer comes back
Winds burst, then drop
Flowers, leaves and colours, nothing's left to hint her
Spring, Summer, Autumn's, withered into winter
(J. C., *Later Poems*, p. 221.)

And for the folkish ballad lyricism:

Love, meet me in the green glen,
   Beside the tall elm-tree;
Where the sweetbrier smells so sweet agen,
   There come with me,
     Meet me in the green glen.

Meet me at the sunset
   Down in the green glen,
Where we've often met
   By hawthorn-tree and foxes' den,
     Meet me in the green glen.   etc.
(J. C., *Mad.*, p. 209.)

As for some letters to his son,

                    Northampton Asylum April 2, 1849
MY DEAR SON CHARLES

    I am happy to hear from you at any time but more particularly now as I am quite lost in reveries & false hums I am now in the ninth year of my captivity among the Babylonians & any news from Home is a Godsend of blessing....
(J. C., *Letters*, p. 300.)

                    Northampton Asylum Nov 7th, 1849
MY DEAR CHARLES

    ....You never tell me my dear Boy when I am to come Home I have been here Nine years or Nearly & want to come Home very much....Have you four Boys got

each an Hebrew Bible & a Harry Phillips on Angling—
How do you get on with the Flowers—how are your Sisters & your Mother & Grandfather your Three Brothers
& your Neighbours Give my Love to them all & Helpston
People likewise—Take care of my Books & M. S. S. till I
come—to your Neighbours on each side of you give my
best respects—& to Mary Buzley & old Mr Buzley if alive
—& believe me my dear Son

Your Affectionate Father
JOHN CLARE

(J. C., *Letters*, pp. 303-304.)

Rural, humble, remote, and impoverished as he certainly was, Clare was by no means illiterate, even if he cared not overly for spelling or "that awkward squad of pointings called commas colons semicolons etc." (Or, as he said another time, "I may alter but I cannot mend grammer in learning is like tyranny in government—confound the bitch I'll never be her slave....)
(J. C., *Letters*, p. 133.)

Clare read widely—the *Bible*, Pope, the eighteenth century English poets, and his own Romantic contemporaries. He was versed thoroughly in Shakespeare, and knew especially *Macbeth* exceedingly well. On diverse occasions, Clare wrote:

> *Sun. 17 Oct. 1824* ....read some passages in my Shakspear took a walk the hedges look beautiful with their hips & glossy sloes lookd into the poems of Coleridge Lamb & Lloyd Coleridge's monody on Chatterton is beautiful....
> (J. C., *Prose*, p. 115.)

> *Wed. 10 Nov. 1824.* Read "Macbeth" what a soul-thrilling power hovers about this tradegy I have read it over about 20 times & it chains my feelings still to its persual like a new thing it is Shakespears masterpiece....
> (J. C., *Prose*, p. 121.)

On another occasion, Clare mentions Robert Herrick, noting that there was on the wrapping paper for plants he had been sent "a fine quotation from Herrick for a Motto how delightful is the freshness of these old poets it is meeting with green spots in deserts."
(J. C., *Prose*, p. 141.)

At times we do find verse by Clare which is melodiously reminiscent of an earlier century:

The crow sat on the willow

The Crow sat on the willow tree
A lifting up his wings
And glossy was his coat to see
And loud the ploughman sings
I love my love because I know
The milkmaid she loves me
And hoarsely croaked the glossy crow
Upon the willow tree
I love my love the ploughman sung
And all the field w' music rung

I love my love a bonny lass
She keeps her pails so bright
And blythe she t[r]ips the dewy grass
At morning and at night
A cotton drab her morning gown
Her face was rosey health
She traced the pastures up and down
And nature was her wealth
He sung and turned each furrow down
His sweethearts love in cotton gown

My love is young and handsome
As any in the Town
She's worth a Ploughman's ransom
In the drab cotton gown
He sung and turned his furrows o'er
And urged his Team along
While on the willow as before
The old crow croaked his song
The ploughman sung his rustic Lay
And sung of Phebe all the day

The crow was in love no doubt
and wi a many things
The ploughman finished many a bout
And lustily he sings
My love she is a milking maid
Wi red and rosey cheek
O' cotton drab her gown was made
I loved her many a week
His milking maid the ploughman sung
Till all the fields around him rung

(J. C., *Selections*, pp. 228-229.)

He felt a special kinship, too, to the work of Thomson—to *The Seasons*—as well as for Cowper. And in the case of Byron, it was perhaps the show of freedom, as well as the lyrical quality, that attracted Clare. Clare was thoroughly aware of the work and the fortunes of John Keats through their mutual publisher, John Taylor. Clare conceived of Keats as,

> ...a brother wanderer in the rough road of life & as one whose eye picks now & then a wild flower to cheer his solitary way who looks with his wild vain & crackd braind friend to the rude break neck hill where sits the illustrious inspirer—Fame—...I judge colors by complexion & for his feeling his love for nature & his genius I heartily love him—I like the extracts from his poems & wait their publication anxiously....[10]
>
> (J. C., *Letters*, pp. 51-52.)

And on having read Keats's *Lamia, Isabella, and other Poems*, published by Taylor and Hessey in July, 1820, Clare wrote:

> I began on our friend Keats new Vol—find the same fine flowers spread if I can express myself in the wilderness of poetry—for he launches on the sea without compass—& mounts pegassus without saddle or bridle as usual & if those cursd critics coud be shood out of the fashion wi their rule & compass & cease from making readers believe a Sonnet cannot be a Sonnet unless it be precisly 14 lines & a long poem as such unless one first sits down to wiredraw out regular argument & then plod after it in a regular manner the same as a Taylor cuts out a coat for the carcass...
>
> (J. C., *Letters*, p. 56.)

It is worth observing that Clare, the most truly rural of all English poets, bridled at the more extravagant vagaries of Keats's Romantic fancy:

> He [Keats] keeps up a constant alusion or illusion to the grecian mythology & there I cannot follow—yet when he speaks of woods Dryads & Fawns are sure to follow & the brook looks alone without her naiads to his mind yet the frequency of such classical accompaniment make it wearisome to the reader where behind every rose bush he looks for a Venus & under every laurel a thrumming Appollo—In spite of all this his descriptions of scenery are often very fine but as it is the case with other inhabitants of great cities he often described nature as she ap-

peared to his fancies & not as he would have described her had he witnessed the things he describes....
(J. C., *Prose*, p. 223.)

In fact, of the idealized pastoral mode in general, Clare had his own views:

> Pastoral poems are full of nothing but the old thread bare epithets of "sweet singing" "love lorn nightingale" "fond turtles" "sparkling brooks" "green meadows" "leafy woods" etc etc these make up the creation of Pastoral and descriptive poesy and every thing else is reckond low and vulgar in fact they are too rustic for the fashionable or prevailing system of rhyme till some bold inovating genius rises with a real love for nature and then they will no doubt be considered as great beautys which they really are
>
> (J. C., *Selections*, p. 114.)

Well might Clare, the scrupulous naturalist, have taken the exception he did to the liberties taken with nature by urban poets of extravagant imagination. For unclouded precision of nature description, consider any random journal jottings of John Clare:

> NIGHT JAR
> not common here (see letter on Fern Owl) but found on Emmonsals heath they make a carless nest of loose grass on the ground & lay 3 eggs not unlike the wood owls of a yellowish white blotted largly with dark spots
> (J. C., *Prose*, p. 279.)

> Sat. Nov. 1824. Recievd a parcel of Ferns & flowers from Henderson the common polipody growing about the Thorp Park wall the harts tongue growing in a well at Caistor the Lady fern growing at Whittlesea Meer & tall White Lychnis with 7 new sorts of Chrysanthemums—the Paper White the bright lemon 3 sorts of lilac & 2 others— I love these flowers as they come in the melancholy of nature
> (J. C., *Prose*, p. 126.)

> Tues. 14 Dec. 1824. A coppled crownd Crane shot at Billings's pond in the green—'Twas 4 foot high from the toes to the bill on the breast & rump was a thick shaggy down full of powder which seem to be a sort of pounce-box to the bird to dress its feathers with to keep out the wet its neck & breast were beautifully staind with streaks

> of watery brown its wings & back was slate-grey the
> down on its head was of the same color
> (J. C., *Prose*, p. 127.)

But we must not think of John Clare merely as one of those whimsical English bird-watchers the culmination of whose activity is the annual list of sightings. He could put his familiarity with nature to relatively sophisticated literary use. Once, for example, Clare sent Taylor some "rustic" verse, which Taylor thought derivative of Wordsworth. Clare responded:

> Do you mistake my imitation of W. W. as a serious attempt in his manner—twas written in ridicule of his affectations of simplicity—& I had thoughts of imitating the styles of all the living poets as I got hold of them to read them nor has the thought left me yet—Southey & Crabb I fancy I can do to a tittle the ones affectation in mouthing over big words the others tedious prosings over trifels often border on the ridiculous though they are both great men & geniuses as I venerate & esteem.
> (J. C. *Letters*, p. 133.)

Clare's keen perceptions were not relegated solely to his notebooks and prose journals. Both in the asylum years, during which he wrote poems such as "Morning," and much earlier, in happier times, when he wrote *The Shepherd's Calendar*, Clare saw Nature with clarity and with exact awareness.

Morning

The morning comes—the drops of dew
Hang on the grass and bushes too
The sheep more eager bite the grass
Whose moisture gleams like drops of glass
The hiefer licks in grass and dew
That makes her drink and fodder too
The little bird his morn song gives
His breast wet with the dripping leaves
Then stops abruptly just to fly
And catch the wakened butterfly
That goes to sleep behind the flowers
Or backs of leaves from dews and showers
The yellow hammer haply blest
Sits by the dyke upon her nest
The long grass hides her from the day
The water keeps the boys away

The morning sun is round and red
As crimson curtains round a bed

The dew drops hang on barley horns
As beads the necklace thread adorns
The dew drops hang wheat ears upon
Like golden drops against the sun
Hedge-sparrows in the bush cry 'tweet'
O'er nests larks winnow in the wheat
'Till the sun turns gold and gets more high
And paths are clean, and grass gets dry
And longest shadows pass away
And brightness is the blaze of day
(J. C., *Later Poems*, pp. 167-168.)

The Shepherd's Calendar, in the tradition of poems on the rural year, demonstrates Clare's empathetic and comprehensive observation in a manner reminiscent of Breughel.

from "January • A Winters Day"

The ickles from the cottage eaves   ickles = icicles
Which cold nights freakish labour leaves
Fret in the sun a partial thaw
Pattring on the pitted snow
But soon as ere hes out of sight
They eke afresh their tails at night
The sun soon creepeth out of sight
Behind the woods—and running night
Makes haste to shut the days dull eye
And grizzles oer the chilly sky
Dark deep and thick by day forsook
As cottage chimneys sooty nook
While maidens fresh as summer roses
Joining from the distant closes
Haste home wi yokes and swinging pail
And thresher too sets by his flail
And leaves the mice at peace agen
To fill their holes wi stolen grain
And owlets glad his toils are oer
Swoops by him as he shuts the door
The shepherd seeks his cottage warm
And tucks his hook beneath his arm
And weary in the cold to roam
Scenting the track that leadeth home
His dog wi swifter pace proceeds

And barks to urge his masters speed
Then turns and looks him in the face
And trotts before wi mending pace
Till out of whistle from the swain
He sits him down and barks again
Anxious to greet the opend door
And meet the cottage fire once more
The robin that wi nimble eye
Glegs round a danger to espy
Now pops from out the opend door
From crumbs half left upon the floor
Nor wipes his bill on perching chair
Nor stays to clean a feather there
Scard at the cat that sliveth in
A chance from evenings glooms to win
To jump on chairs or tables nigh
Seeking what plunder may supply
The childerns litterd scrips to thieve
Or aught that negligence may leave
Creeping when huswives cease to watch
Or dairey doors are off the latch
On cheese or butter to regale
Or new milk reeking in the pale
J. C., *Shepherd's Cal.*, pp. 7-8.)

In contrast to most of Clare's work which this volume displays, "The Badger," and "The Hedgehog" are two poems by John Clare which *are* well-known. Their fame is deserved for, like few other poems, they demonstrate Clare's exact observation, his clear-eyed lack of sentimentality, his compassion, and what seems to me his very pervasive sense of foreboding.

The Badger

The badger grunting on his woodland track
With shaggy hide and sharp nose scrowed with black
Roots in the bushes and the woods and makes
A great hugh burrow in the ferns and brakes
With nose on ground he runs a awkard pace
And anything will beat him in the race
The shepherds dog will run him to his den
Followed and hooted by the dogs and men
The woodman when the hunting comes about
Go round at night to stop the foxes out
And hurrying through the bushes ferns and brakes

Nor sees the many hol[e]s the badger makes
And often through the bushes to the chin
Breaks the old holes and tumbles headlong in

When midnight comes a host of dogs and men
Go out and track the badger to his den
And put a sack within the hole and lye
Till the old grunting badger passes bye
He comes and hears they let the strongest loose
The old fox hears the noise and drops the goose
The poacher shoots and hurrys from the cry
And the old hare half wounded buzzes bye
They get a forked stick to bear him down
And clapt the dogs and bore him to the town
And bait him all the day with many dogs
And laugh and shout and fright the scampering hogs
He runs along and bites at all he meets
They shout and hollo down the noisey streets

He turns about to face the loud uproar
And drives the rebels to their very doors
The frequent stone is hurled where ere they go
When badgers fight and every ones a foe
The dogs are clapt and urged to join the fray
The badger turns and drives them all away
Though scarcly half as big dimute and small
He fights with dogs for hours and beats them all
The heavy mastiff savage in the fray
Lies down and licks his feet and turns away
The bull dog knows his match and waxes cold
The badger grins and never leaves his hold
He drive[s] the crowd and follows at their heels
And bites them through the drunkard swears and reels

The frighted women takes the boys away
The blackguard laughs and hurrys on the fray
He tries to reach the woods a awkard race
But sticks and cudgels quickly stop the chace
He turns agen and drives the noisey crowd
And beats the many dogs in noises loud
He drives away and beats them every one
And then they loose them all and set them on
He falls as dead and kicked by boys and men
Then starts and grins and drives the crowd agen
Till kicked and torn and beaten out he lies
And leaves his hold and cackles groans and dies

Some keep a baited badger tame as hog
And tame him till he follows like the dog
They urge him on like dogs and show fair play
He beats and scarcely wounded goes away
Lapt up as if asleep he scorns to fly
And siezes any dog that ventures nigh
Clapt like a dog he never bites the men
But worrys dogs and hurrys to his den
They let him out and turn a harrow down
And there he fights the host of all the town
He licks the patting hand and trys to play
And never trys to bite or run away
And runs away from noise in hollow trees
Burnt by the boys to get a swarm of bees
(J. C., *Selections*, pp. 126-128.)

"The Hedgehog" is, like "The Badger," a crowded canvas. (Indeed, the canvas metaphor is an apt one to describe these poems which, in one way, resemble paintings of children or "primitives." Much of the richness of such pictures may be attributed to the fact that every inch of the surface is covered with paint and ornament, giving the viewer a sensation of what in the Middle Ages was termed "plenitude," a universe in which all things creatable have been created, a universe without a white background, as it were.)

The Hedgehog

The hedgehog hides beneath the rotten hedge
And makes a great round nest of grass and sedge
Or in a bush or in a hollow tree
And many often stoops and say they see
Him roll and fill his prickles full of crab[s]
And creep away and where the magpie dabs
His wing at muddy dyke in aged root
He makes a nest and fills it full of fruit
On the hedge bottom hunts for crabs and sloes
And whistles like a cricket as he goes
It rolls up like a ball or shapeless hog
When gipseys hunt it with their noisey dogs
Ive seen it in their camps they call it sweet
Though black and bitter and unsavoury meat

But they who hunt the field for rotten meat
and wash in muddy dyke and call it sweat [*sic*]
And eat what dogs refuse where ere they dwell
Care little either for the taste or smell

> They say they milk the cows and when they lye
> Nibble their fleshy teats and make them dry
> But they whove seen the small head like a hog
> Rolled up to meet the savage of a dog
> With mouth scarce big enough to hold a straw
> Will neer believe what no one ever saw
> But still they hunt the hedges all about
> And shepherd dogs are trained to hunt them out
> They hurl with savage force the stick and stone
> And no one cares and still the strife goes on
> (J. C., *Selections*, p. 131.)

"The Hedgehog" is not the equal of "The Badger," if only because of the relative chaos wrought by Clare's vague pronoun references. Not that ambiguous "they's" destroy the poem, which, if anything, teems with an excess of life partly brought on by these same vague "they's." Still, though, it is not immediately self-evident at what point Clare switches subject and object references. However, the vague pronoun references seem to enhance Clare's meaning, suggesting a moiling confusion of men and hounds besetting the poor, small creature. And the last line— "And no one cares and still strife goes on"—also is remarkable, though perhaps partly by accident. Precisely Clare's *lack* of terminal punctuation at the end of the line, which is also the end of the poem, seems to mirror the continuation of the strife that "goes on." Neither the strife has an end, nor does the poem itself. Nor does, we are tempted to say, the fearful universe, nor the misery of the helpless—the badgers, the hedgehogs, "the fly or beetle on their track," who "whemble on their back" in terror.

To summarize, then, Clare's poetical output is large. Much of it is nostalgic, harkening back to a happier time which, in fact, was already passing before Clare grew old enough to observe it, before the land was divided, subdivided, and, in many cases, taken from those who had for centuries tended it. Clare's subjects are the green and peaceful land that England was, the folk, their customs, their labors, their animals, and all the woods and wilds, the birds, the fish, the insects. Much of Clare's verse is sustainedly lyrical and displays metrical facility; some is fliply or scurrilously sardonic, emulating (somewhat implausibly) a Byronic mysogyny. Clare's verse is, at times, incoherent. A good deal is fragmentary. But generally, pervasively, the congenial subject for Clare is the natural world which gave the poet what solace and shelter he was able to find. Some of the poetry, both from the earlier years, and from the years in the asylum too, is of high excellence.

Not only Clare's poetry, but his prose, too, evidences Clare's sympathy and compassion for virtually all life. An odd little piece titled "House or Window Flies" will serve to demonstrate:

> These little indoor dwellers, in cottages and halls, were always entertaining to me; after dancing in the window all day from sunrise to sunset they would sip of the tea, drink of the beer, and eat of the sugar, and be welcome all the summer long. They look like things of mind or fairies, and seem pleased or dull as the weather permits. In many clean cottages & genteel houses, they are allowed every liberty to creep, fly, or do as they like: and seldom or ever do wrong. In fact they are the small or dwarfish portion of our own family, and so many fairy familiars that we know and treat as one of ourselves.
> (J. C., *Prose*, p. 251.)

Clare's tone may remind one of the benevolent Uncle Toby, who addresses a caught fly: "—'Go,—go poor devil,...—get thee gone, —why should I hurt thee? This world is surely wide enough to hold both thee and me.'" (Lawrence Sterne, *Tristram Shandy*, Chapter IV.)

Similarly, when Clare turned his poetical sentiments to the robin, he wrote a kindly cameo:

[The Robin]

Again the robin waxes tame
And ventures pitys crumbs to claim
Picking the trifles off the snow
Which dames on purpose daily throw
And perching on the window sill
Where memory recolecting still
Knows the last winters broken pane
And there he hops and peeps again.
(J. C., *Selections*, p. 132.)

It remains, now, to explain the title of this slender volume. My "Homage," written in poetry, is a "critical correspondence." It is "critical" in that it attempts to shine light on Clare. It is a "correspondence" both in that it is an exchange of messages between us, and in that my own replies are designed to correspond to—to be in the spirit of—Clare, himself. A few of the characteristics which have moved me, which I have found in this very particular friend, as I perceive him, are:

that, though Clare may occasionally remind one of other so-called "peasant poets"—Robert Bloomfield or Stephen Duck—such affinity is superficial. The profundity and the tragedy of John Clare and of his life are singular.

that Clare's nature observations are as perceptive as those of Gilbert White, sometimes as whimsical as those of Sir Thomas Browne, and are touched by a melancholy reminiscent of the writings of W. H. Hudson.

that Clare's letters mirror eloquently a long life intensely felt.

Finally, it seems to me that Clare's poetry is the distillate of observations, ruminations, passions, or joyous lyricism and depressive obsessions of one of the most vulnerable sensibilities in English poetry.

Notes

[1] For editions used, see page x. Eric Robinson and Geoffrey Summerfield announce a projected edition of Clare's poetry in the Oxford English Text Series. *Clare: Selected Poems and Prose*, p. 45.

[2] Albert C. Baugh et al., eds., *A Literary History of England: The Nineteenth Century and After (1789-1939)* (New York: Appleton-Century-Crofts, 1967), IV, p. 1262.

[3] Harold Bloom, *The Visionary Company*, rev. and enlarged ed. (New York: Doubleday, 1961).

Mark Storey, *The Poetry of John Clare: A Critical Introduction* (New York: St. Martin's Press, 1973).

Janet M. Todd, *In Adam's Garden: A Study of John Clare* (Gainesville: University of Florida Press, 1973).

[4] November, 1976.

[5] Sandra McPherson, "Homage to John Clare," *Radiation* (New York: The Ecco Press, 1973), pp. 11-13. I was not aware of McPherson's poem when I named my work.

Jon Anderson, "John Clare," in *The American Poetry Anthology*, ed. Daniel Halperin (New York: Avon Books, 1975), pp. 7-8.

Mark Halperin, "John Clare," *Backroads* (University of Pittsburgh Press, 1976), p. 53.

[6] Theodore Roethke, *The Collected Poems* (New York: Doubleday, 1966), p. 228.

[7] As John Clare stated more than once, he had little use for correctness in spelling or punctuation.

[8] During the asylum years there was a period of time during which Clare would capitalize the initial letters of words; later he would write in a code omitting all vowels. In 1860—very late in his life, when much of his reason had deserted him—he attributed his inability to write to the fact that "they have cut off my head, and picked out all the letters of the alphabet—all the vowels and consonants—and brought them out through my ears; and then they want me to write poetry! I can't do it." (Quoted in Geoffrey Grigson's *Poems of John Clare's Madness*, p. 48.)

[9] Regarding Clare's choice of *Don Juan*, Clare's editors have pointed out "that one of the favorite literary exercises of the later 1820s and the 1830s was to write a continuation of *Don Juan*," and that Clare had an example of such a composition in his own library. (E. Robinson and G. Summerfield, *The Later Poems*, p. 24.)

As for *Child Harold*, Mark Storey has written: "Anyone who has handled the small notebook which Clare carried with him on his long trek home—the notebook crammed full of rough workings, prayers for his family, written wherever he found somewhere to sleep for the night, the diary of that very trek,—can no longer view the poem objectively: the experience out of which it grew is too harrowing." (*The Poetry of John Clare*, p. 159.)

[10]"I judge colors by complexion..." John Clare frequently did deem color significant, but he was not the first English poet to do so. Christopher Smart (1722-1771), who occasionally bears comparison to Clare, and who well may have had Isaac Newton's revolutionary discoveries with prisms in mind, wrote, "Now that colour is spiritual appears inasmuch as the blessing of God upon all things descends in colour." ("Jubilate Agno," section XIX, line 18, in Norman Callan, ed., *Christopher Smart: The Collected Poems* (Cambridge: Harvard University Press, 1949), p. 310.)

[11]Clare loved such lore. In *The Shepherd's Calendar* he wrote:

Old customs O I love the sound
However simple they may be
What ere wi time has sanction found
Is welcome and is dear to me
Pride grows above simplicity
And spurns it from her haughty mind
And soon the poets song will be
The only refuge they can find

The shepherd now no more afraid
Since custom doth the chance bestow
Starts up to kiss the gigling maid
Beneath the branch of mizzletoe
That neath each cottage beam is seen
Wi pearl-like-berrys shining gay
The shadow still of what hath been
Which fashion yearly fades away
(from J. C., *Shepherd's Cal.*, p. 126.)

HOMAGE TO JOHN CLARE:

A Poetical and Critical Correspondence

To the Reader

1. This volume is a *Homage*, a tribute, written in *poetry*. It is once in a great while *critical* in the sense of "admonitory." Usually it is *critical* in the sense that it is intended to shed light on its subject. It is a *correspondence* in the sense that it is "answers to…" and in the sense that it is "in the spirit of…."

2. Clare's poems are on left-hand pages; answers on facing right pages.

3. There exists no complete critical edition of Clare. I have used whatever texts were handiest, or produced a response.

4. Clare uses many dialect words often glossed. I have not glossed them because I think they're perfectly clear in context (e.g. "whemble")—except that one should know that "pooties" are snails.

5. Clare, as I said in the Introduction, does not hold much truck for spelling and punctuation. Hence probably 99% of the errors in Clare's text, following, are in the original, and are not typographical errors.

6. Sometimes, as in the poem with "flyeing mirrors," Clare sees with intense but distorted vision. As a poem came closer to me, I would come to see with what I feel to be a similar distortion, and would attempt to render the distortion in my own poem.

   I have generally strived for simplicity without coyness, in keeping with what I feel about Clare. Sometimes I, too, have eschewed punctuation, or even purposely misspelled (e.g. "childern"). That's simply because Clare's influence was obviously strong.

A Favourite Place

Beautiful gravel walks overgrown
With moss and grass little places
the poet sat to write

(Clare)

(J. C., *Later Poems*, p. 108.)
This is the complete poem from MS 110, written in the Northampton Asylum, about 1845.

and, sun drenched, he wrote with the tongue of bird
with the hum of gnat, bee drone
pointed with the bump of June bug,
he wrote with green grass on wet mosses
Torrents of lines, humms, chirrups, chitterings, soughings, and tweets
sparking, seeping, sending the vines honeyed waters
wild words in mounds, in mountains,
daisy heaps, black eyed susans of words
and hedgerows of rhymes
tangle thistle and thorn
fenny stanzas bogged—late—in winter water words.

> But when in all this profusion
> in crazy gardens
> in all these places
> and in all these weeds, with all worlds' words,
> the poet sat to write
> on grass, in little places,
> the moss song stalled the night

Sat. 30 Oct. 1824. Recievd a present of 2 Volumes of Sermons On the Doctrines & Practice of Christianity from Lord Radstock he is one of my best friends & not of much kin with the world the chrysanthemums are just opening their beautiful double flowers I have 6 sorts this year the claret-coloured the buff the bright yellow the paper-white the purple & the rose-coloured lost one—the chocolate or coffee-color—promisd more from Milton

(Clare)

(J. C., *Prose*, pp. 118–119.)

Chrysanthemums The Practice of Christianity
(for Christopher Smart)

The Practice of Christianity
is not of much kin with the world
(no more than Radstock is)
    for it plants chrysanthemums
    for it rejoices in the Lamb
    for it thanks God for double flowers
    for it sees in six colors a reflection of the Glory of the Lord
        claret-color being under the pollen dust on sacramental grape
        buff color being that of nag sleeping standing up
        bright yellow being that of the rays of the morning sun
        paper white being that of the pages of His holy Book
        chocolate or coffee-color being that of the rich earth
                with moiling worms airing
                soil for flowers
        purple & the rose colored one being lost, taken from
                me by Him for the dye in
                His royal robe

Thanks, praises be to the light that makes all colors
Thanks, praises be for the inner light that shapes poems
Thanks, praises be for moonlight, in which my posies glow silver
                in which snails lay silver trails
                      in which some things are transfigured

May gardens of flowers, of chrysanthemums, prosper
May no man, no beast, suffer on account of my garden
May someone see light in dark night for my verses
May sparrows find ample seed in my garden, and flowers still grow
May lost flowers of purple and rose enhance the Glory of His robe
May poems of praise blossom
May chrysanthemums flourish in our dark earth.

Song

I wish I was where I would be
With love alone to dwell
Was I but her or she but me
Then love would all be well
I wish to send my thoughts to her
As quick as thoughts can fly
But as the wind the waters stir
The mirrors change and flye

(Clare)

(J. C., *Selections*, p. 223.)

John Clare's Song for Mirrors

The flyeing mirrors warp the light
that, spark'd in aeons back,
had coursed the centuries of night
imploding through my black.
Sweet Mary Joyce will read my book°
though she be straight and bone
She comforts me with loving look
Though we lie both as stone.

°Mary Joyce, Clare's great youthful love, had died years before. Clare was periodically confused whether she was dead or alove. (I almost wrote "alive.")

The Water Lilies

The Water Lilies, white and yellow flowers,
    How beautiful they are upon the lake!
I've stood and looked upon the place for hours,
    And thought how fine a garden they would make.
The Pleasant leaves upon the water float;
    The dragon-fly would come and stay for hours,
And when the water pushed the pleasure boat,
    Would find a safer place among the flowers.
They lay like Beauty with a smiling face,
    And I have called them "Ladies of the Lake!"
I've brought the longest pole and stood for hours,
And tried for years, before I got those flowers!

                                                    (Clare)

(J. C., *Mad.*, p. 56.)

Like pain in sleep, the water lilies lie,
dry bridges for the hopper, for the fly,
who darts, who scoots from this to that;
The surface of his world is green, is dry
The pond beneath, unplumbed by fly,
His walk is quick, is circumspect
Around this leaf in rapid twitch
Then island hopping—keys and archipelagoes.
The water lilies' sun-lit surface holds,
And underneath—a terror flows.

My Dear John
    I have not heard from you so long—how do you get on—I wrote to your brother Fred a few Days after Christmass and supposed that he was with You keeping the Holiday—"Love one another"—and be a happy Family and I will be as usual when I get oppertunity—for there is no oppertunity for it here there is neither room nor time for pleasure or common sense we are always wrongways—and may we all be wrongways for ever
                      Amen

                                    (Clare)

(J. C., *Later Poems*, p. 16.)

The letter above dates from the period John Clare was in the Northampton General Lunatic Asylum. It demonstrates Clare's attempt to maintain contact with the world outside, and is addressed to his son.

We are always wrongways:
      Up's down
      down's up
      skewed, straight
      and straight 's a'kilt
and may be wrongways for ever
      The world's mad business soon is o'er
      Dear John, Fred
      Snapt snippets in my head
          the lilies of the field
          "Love one another"
          as the Lord loves you
Bream and gudgeon flop not in my creel
more fast than I on the meadows of His Mercy
on sedge, on banks of His bountiful globe
which only me confound, wrongways
                  again
                  again
I, downside up and top's a turtle,
into the minds of those I love
Insinuate my solitude
My great Bafflement
And beg to be remembered in my Jeopardy
with Affection
                  Amen

from "Summer Evening"

Gen the heaves the ladders set
Sly they climb and softly tread
To catch the sparrow on his bed
And kill em O in cruel pride
Knocking gen the ladderside
Cursd barbarians pass me by
Come not turks my cottage nigh
Sure my sparrows are my own
Let ye then my birds alone
Sparrows come from foes severe
Fearless come yere welcome here

(Clare)

(J. C., *Selections*, pp. 60–61.)

Reply*

Elephant for tusks, pit ponies, circus dogs
dancing bears and hunted hares
bass, sculpin, shark, and whales,
birds of paradise with milliners' tails
seals and otter, mink and stoat
all that swim in tide, in moat;
beaver, badger, spider, bee,
all the crawlers trod by me,
egret, mallard, goose for down,
all you teeming underground,
chipmunk, gopher, or the mole
God protect your scrabbly hole.
Earth and world and circus ring,
May your plight Saint Francis bring;
May in rage the Mighty Lord
Send out Michael armed with sword
Block the path to sparrow nest
Leave the tortured beasts to rest
Ring with flares around the mute,
from suff'ring beasts hold off the brute.
    Defend—oh, Heaven—every beast
    And guard, the most, the very least.

---

*The "Reply" owes a debt, too, to Ralph Hodgson's poem "The Bells of Heaven," and its evocation of "tamed and shabby tigers/ And dancing dogs and bears, /And wretched, blind pit ponies/And little hunted hares." Ralph Hodgson, *Collected Poems* (London: Macmillan & Co., Ltd., 1961), p. 75.

from Hesperus

Hesperus! thy twinkling ray
Beams in the blue of heaven,
And tells the traveller on his way
That Earth shall be forgiven!

(Clare)

from Song Last Day

There is a day a dreadfull day
Still following the past
When sun and moon are past away
And mingle with the blast

(Clare)

(J. C., *Mad.*, p. 143.)
(J. C., *Later Poems*, p. 108.)

There is a day a dreadfull day
When beasts who lived in pain
Shall shed their burden, have their say
And the guilty shall arraign.

The hunted fox, the harried hare
The circus bear with chain
And every sparrow caught in snare
Shall mete out fitting blame.

The fighting cock, the tortured bull
The snake trod under foot
The poisoned mole, the burdened mule
No longer will be mute.

This is the day the dreadfull day
When murdered beasts in Heaven
Shall see their God, shall say their say.
    Pray we may be forgiven.

The Universal Epitaph

No flattering praises daub my stone
    My frailties and my faults to hide;
My faults and failings all are known—
    I liv'd in sin—in sin I died.
And oh! condemn me not, I pray,
    You who my sad confession view;
But ask your soul, if it can say,
    That I'm a viler man than you.

                                              (Clare)

(J. C., *Des.*, p. 91.)

Answer

Odd man.
I thought no such thing.
The sin you lived
is primal fault,
and neither you nor I
could anything but wonder
that, in the darkling skies,
where hawk, where sparrow flies,
one stoops, the other dies,
and under un-daubed stone
twined lover sleeps alone.

True Love

True love, the virgin's first fond passion,
    How blest the swain to prove it!
Should Hymen snatch the lucky hour,
    No power on earth can move it.

When death such loving hearts divides,
    And love on earth is blasting;
Firm fix'd the hope in heaven remains,
    Where love is everlasting.

(Clare)

(J. C., *Des.*, p. 181.)
This poem and the one preceding were written when Clare was young. They are from the first edition of his first published volume.

True Love

You do not sound at all convinced
    when love on earth is blasting
That Heav'n enfolds where man leaves off
    with love that's everlasting.

For Heav'n never felt a maid
    as conny-soft as she
Nor Heav'n does not know what bliss
    her kisses were to thee.

from The Winter's Spring

The winter comes; I walk alone,
    I want no birds to sing;
To those who keep their hearts their own,
    The winter is the spring.
No flowers to please—no bees to hum—
The coming spring's already come.

(Clare)

(J. C., *Mad.*, p. 150.)
Written in the Northampton Lunatic Asylum, 1847.

The Winter's Spring: Time Past, Time Present

The winter is the spring
The coming spring has come;
The future's in the present
The song I'll write was sung.

My hope lies in the past
And the flyeing mirrors show
That the first had been the last
And the acorn dropped on snow.

God is all at once.
I seldom call his name,
for winter spring, and life and death
to me are all the same.

Mary Joyce, and acorn cups
are time and light and snow,
and shatt'ring mirrors flareing light
have shown how I must go

Song

O Love is so decieving
Like bees it wears a sting
I thought it true believing
But its no such a thing
They smile but to decieve you
They kiss and then they leave you
Speak truth they wont believe you
Their honey wears a sting

What's the use o' pretty faces
Ruby lips and cheeks so red
Flowers grow in pleasant places
So does a maidenhead
The fairest wont believe you
The foulest all decieve you
The many laugh and grieve you
Untill your coffin dead

(J. C., *Later Poems*, pp. 157–158.)

Answer

Tallyho tallyho

let logic go
for love, it needs no reasons,
The pretty maids, their faces glow
while love it is in season.
If the pretty don't believe you,
what care if foulest grieve you,
And if you're coffin dead,
there's nothing more be said.

So love and kiss and dream the maid
and write the lines a-turvey
and if such japes won't get her laid
let all songs hence be scurvey.

The point, of course, a' muddled is
and addled is the mind
when lovely maids and maidenheads
make Reason's eye go blind.

[no title]

      How hot the sun rushes
      Like fire in the bushes
The wild flowers look sick at the foot of the tree
      Birds nests are left lonely
      The pewit sings only
And all seems disheartened, and lonely like me

      Baked earth and burnt furrows
      Where the rabbit he borrows
And yet it looks pleasant beneath the green tree
      The crows nest look darkly
      O'er fallows dried starkly
And the sheep all look restless as nature and me

(Clare)

(J. C., *Later Poems*, p. 180.)

No Title Either

    Swirls the stars into day
    Starlight brushes the eye
Fish bake on the beaches by mussels
    Skies empty of light spears
    That for years   rushing down
Pascal in his spaces in which I shall drown

    The earth now   crone,
    Womb turning stone,
One reed bending kindly; the wind it shall bless
    my mind   a dune
    blown by winds from the West
And sheep grazing blindly know naught of the Rest

Stonepit

The passing traveller with wonder sees
A deep and ancient stonepit full of trees;
So deep and very deep the place has been,
The church might stand within and not be seen.
The passing stranger oft with wonder stops
And thinks he een could walk upon their tops,
And often stoops to see the busy crow,
And stands above and sees the eggs below;
And while the wild horse gives its head a toss,
The squirrel dances up and runs across.
The boy that stands and kills the black nosed bee
Dares down as soon as magpies' nests are found,
And wonders when he climbs the highest tree
To find it reaches scarce above the ground.

(Clare)

(J. C., *Sel. Poems*, G., p. 172.)

Clare's Stonepit—a sonnet in return

Up's down.
As through the world I go in fevered pace
in ponds I spy in trees the finny race
leap smart to catch the dragon fly aglow
as he darts down to snap on quail below,
and quail below who peck at fallen seeds
blown random from the wind-whip't weeds.
I joy to tread over steeples underground
and hear beneath me grackle-nesting sound;
the stars below, I love to breast the cloud
and feel among my toes the mindless crowd
make sportive jest in winter maypole dance
and scarce a one among them think to glance
beyond the tree-tops, heav'n, and sable sky
where, cloath'd in Mercy's Glory there pass I.

from Decay

O poesy is on the wane
For fancys visions all unfitting
I hardly know her face again
Nature herself seems on the flitting
The fields grow old and common things
The grass the sky the winds a blowing
And spots where still a beauty clings
Are sighing 'going all a going'
O poesy is on the wane
I hardly know her face again

(Clare)

(J. C., *Selections*, p. 204.)

Poesy—the word's antique
Let's dig, see what it may have been
Perhaps 't was like a fibula
a greave, a krater, or an urn
Perhaps it killed, at distance, like a spear
Or held the oil t' anoint the dead
Let's pry, let's dig and let us find
A Poesy hid deep beneath the ground
hard by a Roman wall, or in the swamp,
frayed, decomposing in the light
and we can sew, can rivet, caulk with care
the cracks, the chips where hit by spears
or, careless, dropt in stall or hearth
And we, with patience, keenness, luck
can, if we take the trouble, reconstruct
A Poesy that's oil-tight, firm, bespeaking grace
To show on velvet—in a crystal case.

[Angling]

I came to the flood washd mead or stream and then my tackle was eagerly fastened on and my heart woud thrill with hopes of success as I saw a sizable gudgeon twinkle round the glossy pebbles or a fish leap after a flye or a floating somthing on the deeper water were is the angler that hath not felt these delights in his young days and were is an angler that doth not feel taken with their memory when he is old?

(Clare)

from Angling

None but true anglers feel that gush of joy
That flushes in the patient minds employ
While expectation upon tip toe sees
The float just wave it cannot be a breeze
For not a waver oer the waters pass
Warm with the joyous day and smooth as glass
Now stronger moved it dances round then stops
Then bobs again and in a moment drops
Beneath the water—he with joys elate
Pulls and his rod bends double with the weight
True was his skill in hopes expecting dream
And up he draws a flat and curving bream
That scarcely landed from the tackle drops
And on the bank half thronged in sedges stops

(Clare)

(J. C., *Selections*, pp. 144, 146.)

Angling, a reply

Ha, there you speak to me!
And as you talk of gudgeon and of bream,
I of torpedo pickerel like to dream,
Would take you, Clare, with me to see a fish
That, on the platter, makes a bony dish
But in the pond, among the pickerel weed
where it, relentless, cruising, loves to feed
Oh Clare, this fish a finny dragon seems
which would devour your gentle English breams,
prognathous jaw and razor teeth to bite
whatever minnows, mayflies, frogs in sight.
For him, not bobber, but a lure I tie
And cast it among lilies floating nigh.
I let it rest, then twitch it just a hair.
The line is taut. He leaps into the air.
The scaly glittering giant 'gainst the sky—
his beauteous, shivering glory blinds the eye.
He shakes his head, throws off the loathsome hook,
dives in dark waters, finds his reedy nook,
and there, unblinking, waits th' entire day,
nor e'er again is duped by artificial prey.

> John Clare, just once before you die
> Feel, hook, such Glory leaping in the sky.

from The Shepherd Boy

The fly or beetle on their track
Are things that know no sin
And when they whemble on their back
What terror they seem in

(Clare)

(J. C., *Later Poems*, p. 189.)

Thoughts on "The Shepherd Boy"

The men, the women, girls or boys
Have sinned no grievous sin
And yet, how morsled are their joys,
What terrors they be in.

The rat, the midge, the slith'ring snake
Did not ask to be born;
In terrors they at night awake
Having dreamed of being torn.

The terror which so "seems"
is neither "seems" nor "might,"
Their world is knit of shackling dreams
That are knotted in the Night.

Long tailed titmouse and Chaffinch and red cap make a most beautiful outside to their nests of grey lichen Linnets and hedgesparrows make a loose ruff outside of coarse green moss wool and roots the first are like the freestone fabrics of finished ellegance the latter like the rough plain walls of a husbandman's cottage yet equally warm and comfortable within Pinks [chaffinch] use cowhair and some feathers for their inside hanging   redcaps get thistle down   hedge sparrows use wool and cowhair intermixed   linnets use wool and cowhair and the furze linnet uses rabbit down....

(Clare)

(J. C., *Selections*, pp. 147–148.)

Nest of Long Tailed Titmouse and Chaffinch

(for O. and L., as they move to a new house)

The long tailed titmouse and the Chaffinch, tastefully sedate,
Grey on grey, demurely sitting,
Grey lichen—what could be more fitting?
And all utilitarian, serviceable, form and function wed
(The exterior echoes what the heart has said)

> Only inside, of luxury a trace,
> a cow hair hanging over an empty space;
> Yet not like redcaps' thistle down, excessive,
> But understated, quietly expressive;
> Not flashing show for vacuous inside,
> But native fabrics that bespeak a modest pride.
> As yeomen's cottage, cozy, warm,
> Th' inside mirroring outside's charm.

Envoi:

May "finished ellegance" your dwelling grace;
As ever, may your Place
reflect decorum that gives charm
to noble Hearts who keep it warm.

"...my mind is, as it always has been from a boy—a disappointment...."

(J. C., *Letters*, p. 296.)
(from a letter written by Clare in the Northborough Asylum, 1841.)

We are not what we would be,
there's the rub
the clay that forms us seems unfired;
it crumbles where it's tapped
and sanity to madness, like the shell to egg,
a fragile house (as someone was to say)
      elusive, as I misremember much,
      I say HOLD ON   HOLD ON
      lobelia, hyacinth
      horehound, thistlebush
      hare, fox, hound,
      bluebells & ferns
      "5 eggs of greenish ash color thickly
            freckeled with browny spots"°
      plover, rail, and watercraik
      Oh, glory, Lord,
      what hues and chatterings
      what silver rivulets
      cave in the brakes, the banks of mind
      till all's a prayer praised skelter
      rainbow hue
      chittering   gobbling
      tweeting languages of larking
      I have lost, but recognize the tone.
The vesicles, the fibers of my mind are crossed,
my mind is as it always has been from a boy;
I know no syntax,
only feel the Acclamation, Praises, Joy

°From J. C., *Prose*, p. 268.

Song

I hid my love when young while [until] I
Coudn't bear the buzzing of a flye
. . . .

I hid my love in field and town
Till e'en the breeze would knock me down
The Bees seemed singing ballads o'er
The flyes buzz turned a Lions roar
And even silence found a tongue
To haunt me all the summer long
The riddle nature could not prove
Was nothing else but secret love

(Clare)

(J. C., *Selections*, p. 226.)
Written in the Northampton Asylum in 1844 or 1845.

There is a secret prudence cannot cure
    I see the murmur of the rocks
    the audible knotting of the roots,
    am deafened as the raindrop
    plashes stone. Tympanum torn
    by nudging mole nose making hillocks
    in sweet tubered loam
    all earth conspires, I am never alone,
    am girdled, garlanded in tunes
    of fishes, flies, elves even
    in the snarls of hedgerows, limbs of yew
    I hear the sowbug's curléd pill
    whembling down a Lilliputian hill
    am caroled by the midges' song above
    am giddied in cacophonies of love
    I suffer secrets prudence cannot cure.

My dearest Mary Collingwood°

I am nearly worn out & want to hear from you nobody will own me or have me at any price & what have I done do you know what you are in my Debt—kisses for ten years & longer still & longer than that when people make such mistakes as to call me God's bastard & whores pay me by shutting me up from God's people out of the way of common sense & then take my head off because they can't find me it out herods herod....you did visit me in hell some time back but don't come here again for 'tis a notorious bad place worse and worse and we are all turned Frenchmen....

(Clare)

(T., *Life*, p. 386.)

°The letter to Mary Collingwood is written in the code Clare used in the asylum at Northampton about 1850. Clare would omit all vowels, "y," the personal pronoun, "I," "you," and the article, "a." I have used the transcription of the editors of Clare's letters.

The line is Hamlet's
but the voice is Lear's.
I am NOT worn out,
just nearly so,
God's bastard
paid by being shut out of the way
    Pray, Mary, pray and say
    I do not have a Frenchman's heart
    Frenchman's semen sere as snailtracks in the sun,
    the thread of darkling travels dried by light,
    Am not a nothing
headless, heedless now.
I heed.
To every nuance of a weed, a bird, a word
or challenge to my head, I heed,
I am.
And whether Bryron, Clare, or Caunt
I am my head,
and none shall have it off
but they must grapple first with one
grown rainbow in his kisses, and in sun
and fisted as a blacksmith cracking rocks
this head of mine shall not come off
all kisses shall be freely giv'n—not paid
the English robin in the English oak
shall carol our beddings once again
no keeper whores shall interfere,
dare touch our moss, our leafy couch,
and ten years' kisses given in a night

    I tell you, rumour's rank,
    Am not worn out (just nearly so)
    Not yet turned Frenchman, God forbid!
    Am Clare, of oak, knurled knots

    Pray, Mary, stay and pray
    they shall not lop my leafy head

[*from* MS. 110]

The bedlams primrose blooms about
Wi' twenty blossoms on a stalk

(Clare)

(J. C., *Later Poems*, p. 102.)

Bedlams Primrose

The bedlams primrose blooms about
and all about it thorn
I wonder as I walk these paths
into what garden born
The bedlams primrose blooms about
And yet 'tis bedlam still
And though the birds fly in and out
there's fences on the hill.

        I shall not write a glooming verse
        When flowers are about;
        The fences keep the primrose in,
        They keep the mad world out.

from Twilight

Now twilight ceases on the verge of even'
And darkness like a pawl spreads over heaven

(Clare)

(J. C., *Later Poems*, p. 177.)

Sweet is sleep that shields the mind from wire.
Sleep black snow blanket on the thread of blood
that winds its searing course down every limb.
Sweet is the sleep to salve the incised fire.

There is the thin string ribbon scratched in skin
forcing an equipoise between sleep and wake
that makes each fretted muscle snap and shake
the thin blood ribbon that the flesh's tied in.

Cut wire, balm the scrape;
Olive oil, with lily pads lay over
the nettled envelope of fragile skin
and pray once more His killing kindness to escape.

The red-coursed skin-map's all, is all.
O'er all the rest there rests His pall.

[Spenserian stanzas—no title]

Spring comes and it is may—white as are sheets
Each orchard shines beside its little town
Childern at every bush a poesy meets
Bluebells and primroses—wandering up and down
To hunt birds nests and flowers and a stones throw from town
And hear the blackbird in the coppice sing
Green spots appear like doubling a book down
To find the place agen and strange birds sing
We have no name for in the burst of spring

The sparrow comes and chelps about the Slates
And pops in to her hole beneath the Eaves
While the cock piegon amourously awaits
The Hen on barn ridge crows and then leaves
With crop all ruffled—where the sower heaves
The hopper at his side his beans to sow
There he with timid courage harmless thieves
And whirls around the teams and then drops low—
While plops the sudden gun and great the overthrow

(Clare)

(J. C., *Later Poems*, p. 157.)

reply, Spenserian

The Breughel vision set upon the page
The childern wand'ring 'round the quilted scene
The whole a picture of a peaceful age
warmed by the softly glowing sheen
that makes of all a childhood village dream:
    Just see the brook and hear it gently flow—
        but now a hint things are not what they seem;
        the vision shattered by an angry blow.
        And now all life is snuffed in God's great overthrow

from I am

I am: yet what I am none cares or knows

(Clare)

To Charles Clare

Northampton Asylum October 15 1849

My Dear Charles
    ...I very much want to get back & see after the garden & hunt in the Woods for yellow hyacinths Polyanthuses & blue Primroses as usual & go in the Meadows a fishing with Henry Phillips in my Pocket—how are your Brothers & Sisters & your Grandfather & how is your neighbour Robin Smith we used to go & make ourselves "welcome at the Bell" at Stone Brig how is your neighbours Seftons & Bellars & old Green & all the rest of Northborough People & how are they at Helpstone & how is Charles Welsh & Jonas Porter how do you get on with Latin Greek Hebrew & Mathematics—you must not forget learning.... I shall not trouble you with a long letter as it is nothing more than an inquiry after the other I am my dear Children
            Your sincere Father
            JOHN CLARE

(J. C., *Selections*, p. 221.)
(J. C., *Letters*, pp. 302–303.)

thoughts while writing a letter to his son, Charles

The world is not much with us here,
the hyacinths, the Primroses,
all my kin
your brothers, sisters
Robin Smith, my friend
seem very far—so far away
what shall I do but course the narrow circuit of my skull,
rehearse old Meadows, yews, and gypsy days with Mary Joyce
and shun the chasm—nerves to mind—
like hellgorge in my dreams at night

    I AM
I have been told most gently many times.
And when I doubt, I run my finger 'round a snailshell's whorl,
then in the thund'ring hollow of my ear I feel
the same, the snailshell harmony, geometry of spheres.

One part of me is Perfect
and thereby I do know myself the brother of the hare, the
    lark, the bream;
it is the part of me at home with Sefton, Bellars, Porter,
    Welsh & Green
it is the part of me your mother scarce recalls
the reason I would have you study Mathematics, Greek
to find celestial harmony of numbers, syntax
echo symmetry within your body as in course of Stars
and learn all life is Holy, and that, by His leave,
YOU ARE, Dear Charles,
as I am told I AM: Your loving father, poor John CLARE

A Vision

I lost the love of heaven above
I spurned the lust of earth below
I felt the sweets of fancied love
And hell itself my only foe

I lost earth's joys but felt the glow
Of heaven's flame abound in me
Till loveliness and I did grow
The bard of immortality

I loved but woman fell away
I hid me from her faded fame
I snatched the sun's eternal ray
And wrote till earth was but a name

In every language upon earth
On every shore, o'er every sea,
I gave my name immortal birth,
And kept my spirit with the free

August 2nd 1844 (Clare)

(J. C., *Selections*, p. 225.)

reply to Clare's asylum poem "A Vision"

There is no Vision, poor John Clare
And things are worser than you think
The words you wrote are writ on air
The world you saw was on a brink

No martins, martens, pooties, hare
Few yews, few oaks, where poets dream
The poems, like midges, lost in air.
The last vast meadows you have seen.°

There is no Vision, poor John Clare!
A madman dreams an earth spring rite,
a dream that we no longer share.
We whorl into eternal Night.
There is no Vision, poor John Clare.

°Eighteenth and nineteenth century enclosure and parcelling of what had previously been common land meant—among many other things—the disappearance of spacious meadows, great trees, etc. (See Introduction)

from Child Harold

Dull must that being live who sees unmoved
The scenes and objects that his childhood knew
The school yard and the maid he early loved
The sunny wall where long the old Elms grew
The grass that e'en till noon retains the dew
Beneath the wallnut shade I see them still
Though not such fancys do I now pursue
Yet still the picture turns my bosom chill
And leaves a void—nor love nor hope may fill

(Clare)

(J. C., *Later Poems*, p. 55.)

reply

who sees the scenes he knew
and who rests in one place so long
that, if return were in the cards,
he would not rue the wrong?
        Hills   brooks
the city's palling nooks
         chipped   mortar
   gap—
chinks to leave   light
—   the sight
of childhood puzzlement and fear,
and once-glad eyes which, now blear,
are inward grown and long unloved....
Dull must he be who sees, unmoved.

from Don Juan*

Milton sung Eden and the fall of man
Not woman for the name implies a wh--e
And they would make a ruin of his plan
Falling so often they can fall no lower
Tell me a worse delusion if you can
For innoscence—and I will sing no more
Wherever mischief is tis womans brewing
Created from manself—to be mans ruin

(Clare)

(J. C., *Later Poems*, p. 83.)

*During his asylum years, Clare frequently thought he was Byron, Ben Caunt (the famous prize-fighter), or others. (But see also footnote 9, to the "Introduction.")

John Byron Lord Clare—a poultice for his raving

What the pain and what the state so sore
and what Spring fancy in the cockade days
to make you now call woman wh--e?
       "I sing man's ruin" is your theme;
       but "man" and "mankind" are the same
       and Milton, when he scotched their game,
       had Eve lead Adam to a gleam
       and left the land they left a dream.

Oh Byron, Juan, Burns, and Clare,
may pooties,° connies, larks, and hares
divert your sleep if it have cares;
may Marigold, may Rosemarie
be all, if aught, you'll ever see.
May humble bee and toad and cow
be all, if aught, that you hear now.
       John Byron, Child in senses two,
       May balming rains now cherish you.

°"Pooties" are the snails so often collected by meadow-wandering John Clare. He recalled them with fondness in his writing.

[1841]

My Dear Eliza Phillips*
    Having been cooped up in this Hell of a Madhouse till
I seem to be disowned & even forgot by my enemies, for there is
none to accept my challenges which I have from time to time
given to the public I am almost mad in waiting for a better
place & better company & all to no purpose It is well known
that I am a prize-fighter by profession & a man that never
feared anybody in my life either in the ring or out of it—
I do not much like to write love letters but this which I
am now writing to you is a true one—you know that we have met
before & the first oppertunity that offers we will meet
again—I am now writing a New Canto of Don Juan which I
have taken the liberty to dedicate to you in remembrance
of Days gone bye & when I have finished it I would send you
the vol if I knew how in which there is a new Canto of
Child Harold also—I am my dear Eliza
                          Yours sincerely
                          JOHN CLARE

                                    (Clare)

I am: yet what I am none cares or knows
    My friends forsake me like a memory lost,
I am the self-consumer of my woes—

                                      (Clare)

(J. C., *Letters*, p. 291.)
(J. C., *Selections*, p. 221.)

*The editors of Clare's letters point out that we "have no evidence that Eliza Phillips was...an 'old love' of Clare's. She may have been no more than a name...."

In the beginning of the letter to Eliza Phillips, Clare believes himself to be Ben Caunt, the boxer. That does not mean, however, that the first half of the letter cannot be a metaphor as well.

Depression
(Eliza Phillips, 1841)

I am fearless
I pass without challenge among my foes
hurl defiance
pace these corridors, await reply

> Three things I say:
> I am a fighter who has never known defeat;
> I write not often words like this, but you I love;
> I, beside myself, guiding my hand, write Byron's poem.

> Three things I say, in all, are one:
> I fight all fighters, yet none comes.
> I love a figment, I knew well, who never was.
> My own heart's poem is not my own.

You think I do not know these things
You think poor Clare is mad,
> thinks he is Caunt, he loves a shadow, writes another's poems,
> and knows not he is small, is modest married, versifies with limp.

And I reply
I tell you I
AM FEARLESS
PASS AMONG MY FOES
I HURL DEFIANCE
KNOWING I
> I have no core
> I doubt that I am I
> I cannot rhyme
> I cannot love
> I cannot fight
> for I AM NOT
> (Not Caunt, not Byron—and too sapped to Love)
> I seek my refuge where I can
> I have no sense of what I am
> I am unhoused
> filleted, boned
> > I am not I

Song Last Day

There is a day a dreadfull day
Still following the past
When sun and moon are past away
And mingle with the blast
There is a vision in my eye
A vacuum oer my mind
Sometimes as on the sea I lye
Mid roaring waves and wind

When valleys rise to mountain waves
And mountains sink to seas
When towns and cities temples graves
All vanish like a breeze
The skyes that was are past and oer
That almanack of days
Year chronicles are kept no more
Oblivions ruin pays

Pays in destruction shades and hell
Sin goes in darkness down
And therein sulphurs shadows dwell
Worth wins and wears the crown
The very shore if shore I see
All shrivelled to a scroll
The Heaven's rend away from me
And thunders sulphurs roll

Black as the deadly thunder cloud
The stars shall turn to dun
And heaven by that darkness bowed
Shall make days light be done
When stars and skys shall all decay
And earth no more shall be
When heaven itself shall pass away
Then thou'lt remember me

(Clare)

(J. C., *Later Poems*, pp. 108–109.)

After Apocalypse   Outpost

After the dreaded day has come
That swallowed up the past
and very shores are shrivelled scrolls
And I am left the last
And skies that were are past and over
And only I alone
tread lava shore,
I spy and grope a tree like bone
Grown leafless in the night
One tree in a world,
a sky unfurled
rolls out away from me
As far as dry eye sees.

    The baleful day has come
    I stand out here alone
    Nor shall the night winds sway
    Nor shall I curses say
    Nor neither kneel nor pray.

    The skies are empty now.
    No stars light night.
    I stand and neither bow
    nor homage give to fright.

    MAD CLARE I STAND ALONE
    Blood pulse in skin and bone;
    Poor errant mind my Home.

    ✦   ✦   ✦   ✦   ✦

Limed rocks and springes for birds
Seared pinions, dry wells, drouth
The world falls off, the edge falls out.
A flick. An eyeblink.
Nothing holds it back
Starlight songs lose themselves in dark spaces
No echo. love, in aeon night.

The snow worm in the Brain
sheds, showers blinding blizzards
and the inner eye—white
the mind—white
I, John Clare, father, poet,
blinded in the blank white of His cruel kindness
of His damnable, His timeless Mercy.

from The Progress of Rhyme

> The jetty snail creep from the mossy thorn,
> In earnest heed and tremulous intent,
>   Frail brother of the morn,
> That from the tiny bents and misted leaves
>   Withdraws his timid horn,
>   And fearful vision weaves.

(Clare)

(T., *Life*, p. xx.)

to Small Things

No jetty snails upon our paths,
our snails are mottled brown
and some do doubt they have intent
or are on earnest errands bent.

Yet if we grant that folk there be
whose minds are strung askew
it may well be that these converse
with brothers in the dew,
and every insect, every snail
recites its humble tale
in such a wise these honored few
may sometimes hear the grassy sigh
of sluggard crawlers inching by.

No jetty snails upon our paths,
few listeners in our crowd;
our silent snails are mottled brown,
the busy world too loud.

Few poets left so tuned awry
with hearing so acute
they hear not merely gnat and fly
but creatures who seem mute.

Now snail who fearful vision weaves,
it does so all alone;
it moves in silence under leaves,
its friendly poet gone.

Birds' Nests*

'Tis spring, warm glows the south,
Chaffinch carries the moss in his mouth
To filbert hedges all day long,
And charms the poet with his beautiful song;
The wind blows bleak o'er the sedge fen,
But warm the sun shines by the little wood,
Where the old cow at her leisure chews her cud.

(Clare)

(J. C., *Sel. Poems*, G., p. 235.)
*Clare's last poem.

      One
Carry your poems to the wood
Where the cow in the grass chews her cud.
The South glowing warm; one bird alone
And a poet come home.

             Two
   'Tis spring, and yet 'tis fall
   as single blends with all.
   Let old be gleaned, and new be sown—
      A poet coming home.

                 Last message
      Steer clear the sedgy fen;
      You'll not cross it again.
      The spring, the wood, the south glows warm.
      May Homing poet ne'er fear.
          The hedges, chaffinch, and the cow
          Will stay the same for ever now.

I am

I am—yet what I am, none cares or knows;
    My friends forsake me like a memory lost:
I am the self-consumer of my woes—
They rise and vanish in oblivions host,
Like shadows in love frenzied stifled throes
    And yet I am, and live—like vapours tost

Into the nothingness of scorn and noise,
    Into the living sea of waking dreams
Where there is neither sense of life or joys,
    But the vast shipwreck of my lifes esteems;
Even the dearest that I love the best
    Are strange—nay, rather, stranger than the rest.

I long for scenes where man hath never trod
    A place where woman never smiled or wept
There to abide with my Creator God
    And sleep as I in childhood sweetly slept,
Untroubling and untroubled where I lie
    The grass below, above, the vaulted sky.

                                                       (Clare)

(J. C., *Selections*, pp. 221-222.)

to: I am

This is your poem allowing no replies.
Some care, some know, and yet it's true
that in th' abyss behind your eyes
You Are the only one who touches you.
    As shadows, when the sun is gone
    Your friends have left you now alone.

"Into that nothingness of scorn or noise"
What caring message can be sent
To haply summon mossy joys
When all your hope is spent?
    A mote into all Space is dropt.
    John Clare. You are. The poem is stopt.

again, I am

The self-consumer of his woes
eats, like the wolf, his entrails out.
The river flows, the pod seed blows
The solitude admits no doubt
    The grebe-full pond that was of yore
    Dead now, is rubbled rock raw shore

Not Thomson, Cowper, not the best
Those poets who divined the small
Can say a word to give you rest,
Can write a line to lift the pall.

Below, the grass; above, the sky
John Clare, in childsleep may you lie
John Clare, you are, in stillness deep
you are, you are; forever sleep.

letter to Mr. Jas. Hipkins°

Dear Sir
 I am in a Madhouse & quite forget your Name or who you are You must excuse me for I have nothing to communicate or tell of & why I am shut up I dont know I have nothing to say so I conclude
      Yours respectfully
       JOHN CLARE

           (Clare)

(J. C., *Letters*, p. 309.)

°The letter to Jas. Hipkins is the last letter we have by Clare, written after he was twenty years at the Northampton Asylum. The editors of the *Letters* identify Hipkins simply as "An unknown inquirer from the outside world."

thoughts on the Last Letter

I am, yet that I am I scarcely know,
nor why, nor what to say.
    Mares' tail clouds streaming
    feather sky blue oceans in my mind
    and caterpillars inch my heart about
    weave hammocks for the Death's Head Moth
    the minute humming window fly
    the fairy buzzer in my skull,
    these all conspire concerts in my head
    that make me misremember much
    make perhaps one to whom I'm much beholden
    fly my mind, your face a swallowtail,
    a swift, black flitting fork
    fled fast as eyeblink
    I remain, forever
    stone stock still
    Respectfully
    For Ever
    John CLARE